Mindfulness for Students

What if you walked into your classroom to find a room full of students who were working cooperatively with one another, focusing on the day's lesson, and able to regulate their own thoughts and feelings? Learn how to teach mindfulness strategies to your elementary and middle school students to provide a foundation for social-emotional well-being and academic engagement. Based on research and designed to complement any school setting, no matter how busy, the practices in this book will create the groundwork for a positive and productive learning environment. The curriculum covers these five key mindfulness practices:

- Breath awareness
- Body awareness
- Focusing on gratitude
- Kindness toward self and others
- Open awareness

Each chapter includes a detailed lesson plan with suggested wording, as well as support materials (e.g., journal templates, activity sheets, and infographics). These tools, as well as audio recordings of the practices, are also available on our website as free eResources for classroom use (www.routledge.com/ 9781138586550).

Wendy Fuchs, PhD, is an Associate Professor in the Department of Teaching and Learning at Southern Illinois University Edwardsville, where she is the Program Director of the Undergraduate Special Education program. She has notable experience working with educators to implement mindfulness practices in school settings, as well as teaching mindfulness and yoga to children and adults outside of schools. She is a Registered Yoga Teacher (RYT 200) and has extensive training in Jon Kabat-Zinn's Mindfulness-Based Stress Reduction, as well as ongoing training and practice in *vipassana* (insight) and *metta* (loving-kindness) meditation.

Also Available from Routledge
Eye on Education
(www.routledge.com/eyeoneducation)

Passionate Learners:
How to Engage and Empower Your Students, 2nd Edition
Pernille Ripp

Passionate Readers:
The Art of Reaching and Engaging Every Child
Pernille Ripp

The Genius Hour:
Fostering Passion, Wonder, and Inquiry in the Classroom
Denise Krebs and Gallit Zvi

The Passion-Driven Classroom:
A Framework for Teaching and Learning, 2nd Edition
Angela Maiers and Amy Sandvold

What Great Teachers Do Differently:
17 Things That Matter Most, 2nd Edition
Todd Whitaker

Your First Year:
How to Survive and Thrive as a New Teacher
Todd Whitaker, Madeline Whitaker, and Katherine Whitaker

Motivating Struggling Learners:
10 Ways to Build Student Success
Barbara R. Blackburn

Building Executive Function:
The Missing Link to Student Achievement
Nancy Sulla

Mindfulness for Students

A Curriculum for Grades 3–8

Wendy Fuchs

Routledge
Taylor & Francis Group
NEW YORK AND LONDON

First published 2019
by Routledge
711 Third Avenue, New York, NY 10017

and by Routledge
2 Park Square, Milton Park, Abingdon, Oxon, OX14 4RN

Routledge is an imprint of the Taylor & Francis Group, an informa business

© 2019 Taylor & Francis

The right of Wendy Fuchs to be identified as author of this work has been asserted by her in accordance with sections 77 and 78 of the Copyright, Designs and Patents Act 1988.

All rights reserved. The purchase of this copyright material confers the right on the purchasing institution to photocopy or download pages which bear the eResources icon and a copyright line at the bottom of the page. No other parts of this book may be reprinted or reproduced or utilised in any form or by any electronic, mechanical, or other means, now known or hereafter invented, including photocopying and recording, or in any information storage or retrieval system, without permission in writing from the publishers.

Trademark notice: Product or corporate names may be trademarks or registered trademarks, and are used only for identification and explanation without intent to infringe.

Library of Congress Cataloging-in-Publication Data
A catalog record for this title has been requested

ISBN: 978-1-138-58654-3 (hbk)
ISBN: 978-1-138-58655-0 (pbk)
ISBN: 978-0-429-50453-2 (ebk)

Typeset in Palatino
by Out of House Publishing

Visit the eResources: www.routledge.com/9781138586550

Contents

About the Author ....*ix*
eResources ....*xi*

1. *Mynd Time*: A Mindfulness Curriculum Grades 3–8 1
   Definition of Mindfulness 1
   Origin of Mynd Time 2
   Intended Audience for Mynd Time..3
   Rationale for Implementing Mynd Time 3
   Mynd Time *Supports Social-Emotional Learning* 4
   Importance of Establishing a Personal Practice 6
   A Guide to Using Mynd Time..6
      Goals of *Mynd Time*...7
      Instructional Components 7
      Recommended Times for Classroom Practice....................................8
      Falling Awake 9
      Generalization and Maintenance 10
      Practical Solutions to Potential Roadblocks 12
      Parent Involvement...14

   Support Materials
      Parent Letter..17
      Journal Template 18
      Practice Log Template 19
      Bookmarks 20

2. Introduction to Stress and the Brain 23
   Chapter at a Glance..23
   Background Information for the Teacher..24
   Lesson 1: Introduction to Stress and the Brain...25

   Stress and the Brain Support Materials
      Infographic: Upstairs vs Downstairs Brain......................................30

Sources of Stress T-Chart 31
Stress and the Brain Small Group Activity 32

3. Breath Awareness 33
   Chapter at a Glance 33
   Background Information for the Teacher 34
   Lesson 2: Focus on Breath Awareness 36
   Script for Breath Awareness Practice 38

   Breath Awareness Support Materials
   Infographic: Benefits of Deep Breathing 39
   Breath Awareness Small Group Activity 40
   Breath Awareness Certificate 41

4. Body Awareness 43
   Chapter at a Glance 43
   Background Information for the Teacher 44
   Lesson 3: Body Awareness 45
   Script for Body Awareness Practice (The Body Scan) 47

   Body Awareness Support Materials
   Infographic: How Stress Affects the Body 49
   Stress and the Body T-Chart 50
   Body Awareness Certificate 51

5. Focus on Gratitude 53
   Chapter at a Glance 53
   Background Information for the Teacher 54
   Lesson 4: Focus on Gratitude 55
   Script for Gratitude Practice 57

   Gratitude Support Materials
   Infographic: What Good is Gratitude? 58
   Gratitude Practice Certificate 59

6. Kindness Toward Self and Others 61
   Chapter at a Glance 61
   Background Information for the Teacher 62
   Lesson 5: Focus on Kindness 63
   Script for Kindness Practice Toward Self and Others 65

Kindness Practice Support Materials
    Infographic: Kindness 66
    Kindness Practice Certificate 67

7. Open Awareness 69
   Chapter at a Glance 69
   Background Information for the Teacher 70
   Lesson 6: Open Awareness 71
   Script for Open Awareness Practice 73

   Open Awareness Support Materials
    Infographic: Open Awareness 75
    Open Awareness Group Activity 76
    Open Awareness Certificate 77

Epilogue 79

References 81

About the Author

Wendy Fuchs, PhD, is an Associate Professor in the Department of Teaching and Learning at Southern Illinois University Edwardsville, where she is the Program Director of the Undergraduate Special Education program. She incorporates mindfulness practices in each of her college courses to help teacher candidates manage stress and she has earned multiple teaching awards. She has notable experience working with educators to implement mindfulness practices in school settings, as well as teaching mindfulness and yoga to children and adults outside of schools. She is a Registered Yoga Teacher (RYT 200) and has additional certification in teaching yoga to children with disabilities. She has completed extensive training in Jon Kabat-Zinn's Mindfulness-Based Stress Reduction teacher training pathway, as well as ongoing training and practice in *vipassana* (insight) and *metta* (loving-kindness) meditation. She is passionate about empowering others to learn and utilize mindfulness practices to reduce stress and unhelpful habits in order to increase their sense of joy and overall well-being.

eResources

The reproducibles in this book, as well as audio recordings of the practices, are available on the Routledge website as free eResources.

They are indicated in the book by the eResources logo . You can access the eResources by visiting the book product page: www.routledge.com/9781138586550. Click on the tab that says "eResources" and select the files. They will begin downloading to your computer.

Chapter 1

Mynd Time: A Mindfulness Curriculum Grades 3–8

Definition of Mindfulness

There are a variety of definitions and descriptions of mindfulness circulating in the media. Terms such as "awareness" and "being present" are used to describe mindfulness. The *Mynd Time* curriculum uses Jon Kabat-Zinn's definition of mindfulness which is "paying attention in a particular way: on purpose, in the present moment, and nonjudgmentally" (Kabat-Zinn, 1994). There has been a strong emphasis on paying attention in the present moment, but less emphasis on the part of the definition that also talks about doing so in a nonjudgmental way. Paying attention, or bringing awareness to someone or something is part of the process, but it is just as important for students to learn self-compassion, patience, and kindness toward oneself and others.

One major misconception about mindfulness is that it is a relaxation exercise. In many cases, the actual formal practices can induce a sense of calm or relaxation, but that is actually not the main goal. The purpose of formal mindfulness practices is to increase our capacity to be present with whatever is happening in the present moment, whether it is good or bad. If we are able to notice and truly experience our thoughts, feelings and habitual responses, we are in a better position to think and act more skillfully than if we are reactive and unaware. Indeed, sitting still and focusing on our breath or bodily sensations can be quite calming; the real purpose of these practices is to tap into a sense of being "okay" regardless of what is happening in our lives.

Origin of *Mynd Time*

The name "*Mynd Time*" is a play on words that combines the words "my" and "mind" It is a friendly prompt to take time to understand "my" "mind" as a way to support our own well-being. *Mynd Time* offers a simple set of strategies that are easy to learn, practice, and implement in most elementary and middle school classrooms. Many of the concepts and practices in this program align with the foundational components of Mindfulness-Based Stress Reduction (MBSR) program, originally created by Jon Kabat-Zinn, PhD, in 1979 at the University of Massachusetts Medical Center. For nearly four decades, MBSR has been studied and shown to be beneficial to an increasingly large number of individuals facing a wide range of life challenges (i.e., chronic pain, depression, anxiety, and addiction). MBSR is a standardized eight-week program for adults that teaches individuals how to use mindfulness practices to bring awareness to their thoughts, feelings, habits and physical bodies as a path to improve their ability to regulate and respond to all aspects of life, including daily stressors, routine activities, and interpersonal relationships. *Mynd Time* mirrors the foundational concepts of the MBSR program in a reduced, modified format for children in Grades 3–8.

Mynd Time is the culminating product of many years of implementing mindfulness practices in schools and other settings. The field-testing of these practices occurred in elementary and junior high settings, as well as summer camps for young children. Each time the lessons and practices were taught, improvements and modifications were made to the content, scripts, and support materials. This curriculum originated with a sincere wish for educators and students to find joy and ease in their lives through these practices.

Mynd Time focuses on five formal mindfulness practices as a solid foundation for increasing general awareness and self-acceptance. Unlike many books and programs on mindfulness for children that provide numerous classroom activities and lessons on specific aspects of social-emotional learning, *Mynd Time* intentionally provides only a few practices that serve as the groundwork for other social-emotional learning. Additionally, *Mynd Time* is appropriate both for educators who are new to mindfulness practices and those educators who have extensive mindfulness or meditation experience. Finally, the *Mynd Time* lessons include systematic instructions and clear, concise teacher language to support educators as they become more familiar with teaching the mindfulness concepts and practices. The most important underlying concept of the mindfulness practices in *Mynd Time* is one of self-empowerment; the idea that we are all capable of learning how to regulate our internal and external responses to the people and events in our lives. The skill of self-regulation is at the heart of our ability to find joy and peace within ourselves, regardless of external circumstances.

Intended Audience for *Mynd Time*

The mindfulness lessons in this book are appropriate for students in Grades 3–8. While many public and private school teachers will find benefit in integrating these practices into their daily instructional routines, other school personnel such as school psychologists, school social workers, administrators, and other specialists may find benefit in teaching these lessons and practices to students in smaller group settings or even one-on-one. Additionally, people in other settings with students in Grades 3–8 (i.e., afterschool programs, detention centers, group homes) can also teach these lessons and practices successfully.

Rationale for Implementing *Mynd Time*

Teachers are no strangers to the everyday stressors of current public school teaching demands. There is an increased focus on accountability in the form of student assessment, teacher evaluations, changing national standards, and challenging student behavior that often interfere with classroom instruction, not to mention the culture and climate of the entire school. The intent of this mindfulness curriculum is to provide classroom teachers and other school professionals with a foundation in using mindfulness strategies to support their own well-being and the well-being of the students in their classrooms.

Childhood and adult stress is at an all-time high. The American Federation of Teachers (AFT) conducted the 2017 Educator Quality of Work Life Survey of nearly 5000 educators (AFT, 2017). The survey revealed that educators find their work "always" or "often" stressful 61% of the time, twice as high as workers in the general population. Educators report the following job-related sources of stress: constantly changing expectations, the stressful workload, the condition of the buildings where they work, shortage of resources (e.g., time, equipment, staff), the feeling of having to be 'always on,' and insufficient time to collaborate with colleagues (AFT, 2017). Educators also reported having "poor mental health for 11 or more days per month at twice the rate of the general U.S. workforce" (AFT, 2017). It is interesting to note that the majority of the sources of stress occur outside the classroom and do not come from students.

In addition to teacher stress, children in today's schools are experiencing elevated levels of stress and anxiety related to past trauma, excessive time spent on social media, etc. Mindfulness practices have extensive evidence that supports a promising, positive effect on psychological and physical symptoms associated with anxiety, depression, and overall health, as well as improved attitudes about school and increased academic achievement (Durlak et al., 2011; Greenberg et al., 2003; Zins, Weissberg, Wang, & Walberg,

2004). Incorporating mindfulness lessons and practices in the daily routine will not only help students feel more calm and focused, but will also support an overall positive learning environment. Students who feel better about themselves and feel capable of regulating their own internal and external responses will be contributing members of a positive learning community within the classroom.

Time is a precious and limited resource during the school day, so dedicating a few minutes to practices that support general well-being, teachers and students will find that the time spent on "my/mind" time, will create a more calm, focused, and productive learning environment throughout the day. And, like all significant knowledge and skills we teach in school, the most successful and relevant lessons are maintained and generalized into daily life, in and outside of the school building. If students learn these healthy practices and have the opportunity to practice and improve their skills, they are more likely to employ these strategies in their lives beyond the school day.

Mynd Time Supports Social-Emotional Learning

Mynd Time addresses multiple social-emotional learning standards. Some common social-emotional learning standards include important life skills such as identifying and managing one's emotions, recognizing the feelings and perspectives of others, and using social skills to interact effectively with others. Underlying these social skills is the need for self-regulation—not only regulating one's own thoughts and feelings, but also one's actions. *Mynd Time* specifically aims to support students in increasing their self-regulatory skills. In addition to practicing self-regulation, students also increase their awareness of their own minds and bodies, which is a prerequisite to managing one's emotions and actions.

Nearly all fifty states currently have social-emotional learning standards for preschool students. Some states have aligned these standards for preschool up to third grade (Washington and Idaho). Other states, such as Illinois and Pennsylvania, have required Social-Emotional Learning Standards for preschool through twelfth grade that all teachers must teach and assess during the school day.

The Collaborative for Academic, Social and Emotional Learning (CASEL) is the world's leader in researching SEL programs and promoting the integration of academic, social and emotional learning in schools PreK to twelfth grade. CASEL's mission is to help make evidence-based social and emotional learning (SEL) fully integrated into school curricula. The five competencies associated with Social and Emotional Learning (SEL) are:

Table 1.1 Five Social-Emotional Competencies from CASEL

- **Self-awareness:** The ability to recognize accurately one's emotions and thoughts and their influence on behavior. This includes accurately assessing one's strengths and limitations, and possessing a well-grounded sense of confidence and optimism.

- **Self-management:** The ability to regulate one's emotions, thoughts, and behaviors effectively in different situations. This includes managing stress, controlling impulses, motivating oneself, and setting and working toward achieving personal and academic goals.

- **Social awareness:** The ability to take the perspective of and empathize with others from diverse backgrounds and cultures, to understand social and ethical norms for behavior, and to recognize family, school, and community resources and supports.

- **Relationship skills:** The ability to establish and maintain healthy and rewarding relationships with diverse individuals and groups. This includes communicating clearly, listening actively, cooperating, resisting inappropriate social pressure, negotiating conflict constructively, and seeking and offering help when needed.

- **Responsible decision making:** The ability to make constructive and respectful choices about personal behavior and social interactions based on consideration of ethical standards, safety concerns, social norms, the realistic evaluation of consequences of various actions, and the well-being of self and others.

Source: Collaborative for Academic, Social, and Emotional Learning, 2012, *Effective Social and Emotional Learning Programs* (Retrieved from http://casel.org/wp-content/uploads/2016/01/2013-casel-guide-1.pdf)

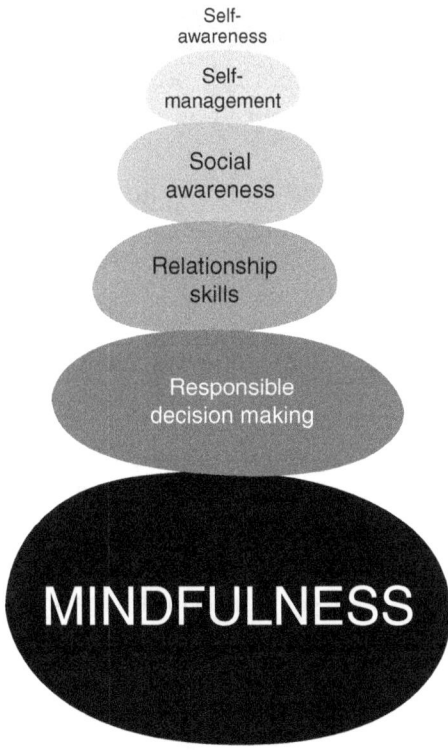

Figure 1.1 Mindfulness as the Foundation to SEL Competencies

Importance of Establishing a Personal Practice

Similar to any other curriculum, it is nearly impossible to teach effectively something if you do not have firsthand knowledge of the subject. We would not expect someone who has no knowledge of physics to effectively teach physics, nor would we ask a person with basic math computation skills to teach calculus. The domain of mindfulness is no different. You will be better able to explain the concepts, understand your students' experience, and continue to learn and grow with your students if you establish your own mindfulness practice first. This does not necessarily require formal training, but it is important that you are comfortable with the terminology, the general concepts, and have some firsthand experience with the practices.

There is no specific practice or amount of time required for a daily practice, but generally, people find at least 10–20 minutes of formal daily practice provides a good foundation for reaping the social, emotional, and physical benefits of mindfulness practices. Everybody is different, and you should find what works best for you. Some people like to practice first thing in the morning as a way to start their day. Other people find that they prefer to do a formal practice right before bed as a way to end their day. We are all busy and finding time to "sit and do nothing" can seem impossible, but if we prioritize our own well-being, the time spent being mindful is the best use of your limited time. The important point is that you practice what you preach. If you think it is valuable for your students to practice mindfulness, then it makes sense for you also to value practicing mindfulness in your own life. You will be more effective in creating a positive learning environment if you are also practicing being more aware and kind along with your students.

A Guide to Using *Mynd Time*

In this book, you will find a mindfulness curriculum that includes five formal practices: Breath Awareness, Body Awareness, Focus on Gratitude, Kindness toward Self and Others, and Open Awareness. Each lesson teaches a mindfulness concept and formal practice that typically takes about 30–40 minutes to: (1) review previously learned information (5 minutes); (2) teach a mini-lesson on the new concept (10–20 minutes depending on the age of the students); (3) discuss the new concept; (4) practice the strategy itself (3–5 minutes), and (5) generalize the concept/practice. Each lesson has supporting materials and suggested websites to provide additional information that will enhance the delivery of the mini-lesson and facilitation of a class discussion. Each mindfulness practice comes with a script to read verbatim or modify to fit your own voice, tone, word choice, or examples.

The *Mynd Time* lessons are an introduction to basic mindfulness concepts and should be retaught or revisited as needed. You will be able to judge how well the students understand the concepts based on class discussion and questions asked. It is also a good idea to have a small group of students who really understand the concepts teach any new students entering the class. Peer tutoring will not only help new students feel more welcomed and a part of the class/community, but will also reinforce the skills and concepts for peers ready to teach the general concepts to other students. Once students master the concepts in the lessons, they will understand the purpose of the daily practice.

Goals of Mynd Time

The major goals of *Mynd Time* are threefold:

1. To assist students in understanding their own minds and bodies.
2. To help students increase their capacity to bring awareness to whatever is occurring (e.g., their own thoughts, feelings).
3. To assist in the development of self-regulation to decrease stress and increase overall well-being, including personal agency and healthy interpersonal relationships.

Instructional Components

The instructional components of *Mynd Time* include reviewing students' background knowledge and connecting that knowledge to new information and practices. In addition, *Mynd Time* uses explicit instruction to teach and model the correct information with appropriate examples for each concept and practice, as well as incorporating small group work and discussion to maximize student engagement. Each lesson concludes with a short explanation of possible ways that the concept and practice applies across settings.

1. *Engage students and activate background knowledge.* Students are more likely to engage in the lesson and remember the concepts if they perceive the information as personally relevant. Each lesson intends to engage students in thinking about the role of stress in their lives, and how the practices may help them. In addition to connecting the content to relevant real-life examples, each lesson activates background knowledge to enable students to tie new concepts to knowledge they

already possess. Students are more likely to retain the information from the lesson if they are able to connect it with concepts and information they already know.
2. *Introduce the new concept.* Teachers are amazing role models for their students. Students will rely on the teacher's experience and knowledge to scaffold their own understanding of the mindfulness concepts and strategies. In each lesson, teachers will provide examples that appropriately address the discussion prompts so that students are able to apply their own experiences in a similar way.
3. *Facilitate small group and whole class discussion.* Learning is a social activity and the more students are able to talk to their peers, reflect on their own knowledge and share ideas with the larger group, the better they will retain the information and see how the newly learned information applies to their own lives.
4. *Practice the strategy.* Talk is cheap, and students will retain information more readily if they are able to process the instructions and practice the newly learned concepts/strategies. Just talking about a strategy for reducing stress is one thing, but to *practice* the strategy with the teacher and class is entirely different. Students have the opportunity to experience the concept, then ask questions and reflect on that experience.
5. *Generalize to other settings.* As mentioned before, the goal of these practices is for students to recall and apply the strategies independently across a wide range of settings. Each lesson will include discussion prompts or language in the actual strategy script that invites students to think about where they might apply, for example, the formal practice of Breath Awareness in various settings throughout their day.

Recommended Times for Classroom Practice

Ideally, after each strategy's lesson presentation, you schedule at least one time per day to practice the strategy as a class (5 minutes). Typically, mindfulness practices work well first thing in the morning, giving the class time to settle into their surroundings, start the day on a positive note, and focus on the tasks ahead. It can also be useful to practice the strategy between transitional times such as right before or after lunch and recess, or right before getting on the bus at the end of the day.

There is no "right way" to practice these strategies. Striving to do the strategies in a certain way is a natural inclination, but does not hold value in the *Mynd Time* curriculum. The purpose of a daily practice is to become more aware of how things are in the present moment, without judging or creating more stress. Moreover, as long as you support this type of practice in the classroom, there are infinite "right ways" to implement *Mynd Time*. In other words, it is a time to check in and ask ourselves, "How does my body feel?" or "What are my thoughts and feelings?" or "What is my current mood?" and then letting the answers arise, without the need to judge or change what comes to the surface. How this happens in each classroom depends on many factors, such as teacher personality, student readiness, group dynamics, classroom environment, etc. These practices are designed to build our capacity for being kind and gentle toward oneself and others, and allows us to respond compassionately and intentionally, rather than react mindlessly, when we experience stress in our lives.

Having said all of this, there are a few things to keep in mind as each educator creates their own routine and environment for practicing. First and foremost, you are a role model, and your attitude toward the lesson activities and the daily practice will undoubtedly influence the students' willingness to try or continue practicing with open minds and hearts. A teacher's preparation and positive, supportive attitude can encourage students to engage in the practices and to investigate aspects of their lives they might not typically explore. Students may be more likely to share their feelings or thoughts if they perceive the classroom environment to be safe and supportive.

Additionally, students may have an easier time focusing on their breath or bodily sensations if the physical classroom is free from distractions, bright lights, and noise from outside the classroom. Consider closing the classroom door, dimming the lights, etc. to create visual and other sensory cues that are associated with a calm, quiet setting. Asking students to focus on their breath can be challenging at first, so providing a safe, quiet environment can contribute to, rather than compete with, the daily practice.

Here are a few sample schedules to follow as students learn the new concepts and practices. Again, there are many "correct" ways to structure the daily practice. The important part is that students understand the purpose of the practices, and have ample time to practice (i.e., daily).

Falling Awake

Each of the formal practices invites students to sit in a particular way. Students need to know that this is intentional. At school, we do not ask students to sit very still, with their eyes closed. It is not a typical school practice, nor is it a common practice anywhere outside of the school setting. Our bodies have learned through many years of practice, that when we close our eyes and become still, it is time to go to sleep. *Mynd Time* teaches students a new way of responding to being still. At first, it is completely natural for the mind and

Table 1.2 Sample Weekly Practice: Breath Awareness (August/September)

Monday	Tuesday	Wednesday	Thursday	Friday
8:30 Attendance then Breath Awareness	8:30–9:00 P.E.	**8:30 Attendance then Breath Awareness**	**8:30 Attendance then Breath Awareness**	8:30–9:00 Computers
8:45–9:45 Math	**9:00 Breath Awareness**	8:45–9:45 Math	8:45–9:45 Math	9:00–9:30 Art
9:45–10:45 Music	9:10–10:15 Math	9:45–11:30 Literacy	9:45–11:30 Literacy	**9:30 Breath Awareness**
10:45–11:30 Literacy	10:15–11:30 Literacy			9:40–11:30 Reading, Spelling Tests & Math Test
11:30–12:30 Lunch/Recess	11:30–12:30 Lunch/Recess	11:30–12:30 Lunch/Recess	11:30–12:30 Lunch/Recess	11:30–12:30 Lunch/Recess
12:30–12:45 Silent Reading	12:30–12:45 Silent Reading	**12:30–12:45 Breath Awareness & Silent Reading**	12:30–12:45 Silent Reading	12:30–12:45 Silent Reading
12:45–3:00 Social Studies/Science	12:45–3:00 Social Studies/Science	12:45–3:00 Social Studies/Science	12:45–3:00 Social Studies/Science	12:45–3:00 Social Studies/Science
	3:00 Before dismissal, Breath Awareness			**3:00 Before dismissal, Breath Awareness**

body to feel tired during these formal practices. Not only have we trained our bodies and minds to go to sleep when we are quiet but many children and adults still do not get enough sleep. Students' feelings of sleepiness are completely understandable. *Mynd Time* teaches students to practice to send a different message to their minds and bodies when they sit in a comfortable, upright, seated position, rather than give their minds and bodies the message that it is time to tune out and go to sleep. Essentially, they are teaching their minds and bodies to "fall awake."

Generalization and Maintenance

Any time the teacher can reinforce the language and concepts in the *Mynd Time* lessons, the better chance there is for students to not only retain the

Table 1.3 Sample Monthly Practice

	\multicolumn{5}{c}{October}
	Monday	**Tuesday**	**Wednesday**	**Thursday**	**Friday**
Week 1	Breath Awareness	Body Scan after P.E. Breath Awareness before dismissal	Breath Awareness a.m. and p.m.	Breath Awareness	Body Scan Breath Awareness before dismissal
Week 2	Body Scan	Body Scan after P.E. Breath Awareness before dismissal	Breath Awareness a.m. and p.m.	Breath Awareness	Body Scan Breath Awareness before dismissal
Week 3 Introduce Gratitude Practice	Focus on Gratitude	Focus on Gratitude Breath Awareness before dismissal	Focus on Gratitude Breath Awareness p.m.	Focus on Gratitude	Focus on Gratitude Breath Awareness before dismissal
Week 4	Breath Awareness	Focus on Gratitude Breath Awareness before dismissal	Breath Awareness a.m. and p.m.	Focus on Gratitude	No School

Table 1.4 Sample Begining of the Year Practice Schedule

Mindful School District #108

2018–19 School Calendar

Key:
Breath Awareness XX
Body Scan XX
Focus on Gratitude (XX)
Kindness Practice XX
Open Awareness XX

August 2018
S M T W T F S
          1 2 3 4
5 6 7 8 9 10 11
12 13 14 15 16 17 18
19 20 21 22 23 24 25
26 27 28 29 30 31

September 2018
S M T W T F S
                    1
2 3 4 5 6 7 8
9 10 11 12 13 14 15
16 17 18 19 20 21 22
23 24 25 26 27 28 29
30

October 2018
S M T W T F S
    1 2 3 4 5 6
7 8 9 10 11 12 13
14 15 16 17 18 19 20
21 22 23 24 25 26 27
28 29 30 31

November 2018
S M T W T F S
            1 2 3
4 5 6 7 8 9 10
11 12 13 14 15 16 17
18 19 20 21 22 23 24
25 26 27 28 29 30

December 2018
S M T W T F S
                    1
2 3 4 5 6 7 8
9 10 11 12 13 14 15
16 17 18 19 20 21 22
23 24 25 26 27 28 29
30 31

January 2019
S M T W T F S
    1 2 3 4 5
6 7 8 9 10 11 12
13 14 15 16 17 18 19
20 21 22 23 24 25 26
27 28 29 30 31

February 2019
S M T W T F S
                1 2
3 4 5 6 7 8 9
10 11 12 13 14 15 16
17 18 19 20 21 22 23
24 25 26 27 28

March 2019
S M T W T F S
                1 2
3 4 5 6 7 8 9
10 11 12 13 14 15 16
17 18 19 20 21 22 23
24 25 26 27 28 29 30
31

April 2019
S M T W T F S
    1 2 3 4 5 6
7 8 9 10 11 12 13
14 15 16 17 18 19 20
21 22 23 24 25 26 27
28 29 30

May 2019
S M T W T F S
        1 2 3 4
5 6 7 8 9 10 11
12 13 14 15 16 17 18
19 20 21 22 23 24 25
26 27 28 29 30 31

June 2019
S M T W T F S
                    1
2 3 4 5 6 7 8
9 10 11 12 13 14 15
16 17 18 19 20 21 22
23 24 25 26 27 28 29
30

July 2019
S M T W T F S
    1 2 3 4 5 6
7 8 9 10 11 12 13
14 15 16 17 18 19 20
21 22 23 24 25 26 27
28 29 30 31

information, but also apply the strategies across multiple settings over time. When students are able to maintain and generalize the practices, they will access their own inner resources and rely less on adults to help them regulate their thoughts, feelings and actions.

It is beneficial to use the terminology associated with the different strategies as cues for students to check-in and monitor their own behavior in a proactive way. An example of generalizing the Breath Awareness strategy might be when the teacher encounters a student who is forgetting to raise her hand before she speaks, the teacher might say, "Take a moment to bring your awareness to your breath. (Pause.) Now think about what you need to do first." Another example of generalizing the Focus on Gratitude strategy could be when a student is having a bad day and cannot think of anything good that has happened. The teacher could prompt the student to take a few moments to focus on people/things he is grateful for, using some of the same language from the strategy script. The more opportunities students have to practice the strategies in addition to the formal five-minute practice, the greater chance they will utilize the strategies appropriately and naturally.

Practical Solutions to Potential Roadblocks

What if students giggle and squirm?
These practices are unlike anything we typically ask students to do. There is very little time for students to talk with each other, reflect on their own feelings, and take a few quiet minutes without any other expectations or demands. At first, sitting still or discussing personal feelings with peers can feel foreign and uncomfortable for students. Keeping this in mind, it is still possible to maintain a respectful learning environment while allowing some adjustment time for students to get used to this new way of being. It is a good idea to acknowledge and validate their feelings or reactions that the formal practices are not the typical way we spend our time at school, but after a period of adjustment, the quiet time will feel more familiar.

What if the students do not close their eyes when prompted?
Closing one's eyes is an option but not a requirement. The wording in the script for each strategy intentionally *invites*, *not requires* students to close their eyes. The purpose of closing one's eyes during the formal mindfulness practices is to limit visual sensory input. By students simply lowering their gaze toward their desks or laps, they can achieve the same effect. It is very important to consider that some students may not be comfortable closing their eyes, especially if they have experienced trauma. Students will still benefit from these practices if they choose to leave their eyes open.

What if I ask students how they felt during the strategy and they say they do not like it or they think it is boring?

Occasionally, it is beneficial to ask the students about their experiences with the practices. There are a few reasons to ask students about their first-hand experience: (1) it demonstrates that the teacher cares about them; (2) it can help answer questions or clear up misconceptions about the practices themselves; and (3) it helps all students hear a broad range of experiences to normalize different perspectives. For example, if the teacher only asks students to share their positive experiences, those students feeling confused or frustrated with the practices may feel like they are not doing something correctly. Rather, if students perceived that some classmates enjoy the practices and feel calm and focused, while other classmates are bored and frustrated, it communicates that any experience is valid.

My schedule is full every single day. How can I possibly add one more thing to our day?

Limited time and resources is the reality in today's schools. There is no doubt that teachers have a multitude of tasks, lessons, and activities to cover each day. Part of what can help with this feeling of adding "one more thing" is to consider the outcome of the time the teacher dedicates to *Mynd Time*. In essence, a few minutes of quiet time at the beginning of the day can cut down on noisy and/or chaotic transition times, help students focus more easily, and reduce the interruptions and distractions during the engaged academic time. The recommendation is to start small. If you can devote 3–5 minutes at the beginning of the day, you may find that you actually have extra time because of shortened transitions and a decrease in interruptions. The teacher may also find that once a routine is established, the students will reinforce the time spent on *Mynd Time* by reminding the teacher if they missed their daily practice, or requesting to practice before a test or major assignment.

How can I practice with my students without having to leave one eye open?

This is a common concern classroom teachers have. *Do not underestimate the power of your example.* Yes, these practices take some getting used to, but if students understand (by your example) that this is an important part of their school day, you may be surprised by their ability to really engage with the practices. There will be students who like to make other students laugh, and others who may be uncomfortable with the silence or stillness. Just as we do not expect students to improve any other skill without practice, we should not expect students to be able to sit still automatically. What we do not want to do is make the mindfulness practices unpleasant because of rigid rules or overbearing supervision.

As educators, we typically give instructions and expect students to follow those instructions in a particular way. Mindfulness practices are *very* different. There definitely need to be classroom rules in place that honor each other's right to their own experiences. So, if students are following the classroom agreements (sitting still, being quiet, trying their best), the rest is open for them to experience in their own way. Keep in mind, even those students who initially show resistance and distaste for the mindfulness practices can learn to be aware of their minds and bodies. Mindfulness practices are not for creating happy thoughts and relaxed muscles. Students who do not like the practices can use mindful awareness to notice their thoughts and feelings and how they may change over time.

Parent Involvement

Whether you intend to start the *Mynd Time* at the beginning of the school year, or at a later date, it is worthwhile to share the rationale and purpose of this program with parents. Some parents may be familiar with mindfulness or possibly even have a personal practice of their own. Other parents or guardians may not have a clear understanding of mindfulness. The lessons and practices in *Mynd Time* are designed to be long lasting and useful across many contexts. For that reason, parents who are aware of the program can support their child's generalization and maintenance of the skills practiced at school. There is a sample parent letter at the end of this section that can be copied and sent home, or modified to fit your style.

Support Materials

Practice Log and Journal Templates

You will find Practice Log and Journal templates at the end of this section if you would like to incorporate more writing activities into the *Mynd Time* lessons. These two templates are also great for students to monitor their own practice and reflections over time.

Bookmarks

There are bookmarks included for each mindfulness practice for you to copy and distribute to your students. Sometimes having a visual cue can support maintenance and generalization of the concepts and practices. Students may also choose to make their own, which is a great way for them to personalize and internalize their understanding of the practices.

Resources on Mindfulness

Books for Educators to Expand their Own Practice
Brach, T. (2003). Radical acceptance: Embracing your life with the heart of a Buddha. New York: Bantam Books.
Brach, T. (2013). True refuge: Finding peace and freedom in your own awakened heart. New York: Bantam Books.
Brown, K. W., Creswell, J. D., & Ryan, R. M. (2015). Handbook on mindfulness: Theory, research, and practice. New York: Guilford Press.
Goleman, D., & Davidson, R. J. (2017). Altered traits: Science reveals how meditation changes your mind, brain, and body. New York: Penguin.
Grenville-Cleave, B. (2012). Introducing positive psychology: A practical guide. New York: MJF Books.
Hanson, R. (2009). Buddha's brain. Oakland, CA: New Harbinger.
Hanson, R. (2013). Hardwiring happiness: The new brain science of contentment, calm, and confidence. New York: Harmony Books.
Kabat-Zinn, J. (1992). Wherever you go, there you are. New York: Hyperion.
Kabat-Zinn, J. (2018). Meditation is not what you think. Boston, MA: Hachette.
Stahl, B., & Goldstein, E. (2010). A mindfulness-based stress reduction workbook. Oakland, CA: New Harbinger.
Salzberg, S. (1995). Loving-Kindness: The revolutionary art of happiness. Boulder, CO: Shambala Publications.

Books on Mindfulness for Children
Hanh, T. N. & Weare, K. (2017). Happy teachers change the world: A guide for cultivating mindfulness in education. Berkeley, CA: Parallax.
Saltzman, A. (2014). A still quiet place: A mindfulness program for teaching children and adolescents to ease stress and difficult emotions. Oakland, CA: New Harbinger.
Vo, D. X. (2015). The mindful teen: Powerful skills to help you handle stress one moment at a time. Oakland, CA: New Harbinger.
Willard, C., & Saltzman, A. (eds). (2015). Teaching mindfulness to kids and teens. New York: Guilford Press.
Willard, C. (2014). Mindfulness for teen anxiety: A workbook for overcoming anxiety at home, at school & everywhere else. Oakland, CA: New Harbinger.

Websites
Calm Classroom: https://calmclassroom.com
Dan Siegel: www.drdansiegel.com
Mindful Schools: www.mindfulschools.org
Mindful Teachers: www.mindfulteachers.org or www.facebook.com/mindfulteachers
Plum Village's Wake Up Schools: https://wakeupschools.org/
Rick Hanson: www.rickhanson.net/how-your-brain-makes-you-easily-intimidated/

Other Information (e.g. Articles, Podcasts, Reports)

The Future of Education: Mindful Classrooms: www.mindful.org/mindfulness-in-education/

18 Amazing Mindfulness Activities for the Classroom: www.teachstarter.com/blog/classroom-mindfulness-activities-for-children/

18 Science-Based Reasons to Try Loving-Kindness Meditation: www.mindful.org/18-science-based-reasons-to-try-loving-kindness-meditation/

American Psychological Association, *Stress in America 2017 Report*: www.apa.org/news/press/releases/stress/

Dear Parents,

I wanted to share some exciting news with you. Next week, we will start our Mynd Time lessons. Mynd Time teaches mindfulness practices as a solid foundation for social emotional well-being. The goals of Mynd Time are: 1) to help students understand how their minds work, and 2) to increase their self-awareness and self-regulation.

Mindfulness is defined as "paying attention, on purpose, in a particular way, in the present moment" (Kabat-Zinn, 1994). Essentially, we are learning how to focus our attention, in a quiet and still way, so that our minds can get a break from all of the thinking and learning they do all day long! Research shows that these practices can have a positive effect on many aspects of our lives, including better relationships with others, feeling better about themselves and others, and improved focus and concentration.

Feel free to ask your child about what they are learning, or to show you how we practice. This is an exciting foundation to our required Social Emotional Learning lessons and we are happy to share. The great thing about these strategies is that they cost nothing, require no extra technology or equipment, and can be done any time, any place.

If you would like more information about mindfulness please let me know. I am happy to share additional resources.

Best Regards,

A+ Teacher

Journal Entry
Date:

_____

_____

_____

_____

Journal Entry
Date:

_____

_____

_____

_____

© 2019 Taylor & Francis

MYND TIME PRACTICE LOG

Date	Practice	Thoughts, Feelings, Comments

BREATH *Awareness*

FEEL YOUR

BREATH

IN YOUR BODY.

IN AND OUT,

IN AND OUT,

JUST LIKE THE

WAVES

IN THE OCEAN.

BODY SCAN

Slowly check in with your body from your feet up to the top of your head.

Be your best SELF!

FOCUS ON Gratitude

o————o

o————o

o————o

Chapter 2

Introduction to Stress and the Brain

Chapter at a Glance

Lesson 1: Introduction to Stress and the Brain

In this lesson, students will learn about the "upstairs" and "downstairs" parts of the brain and their respective functions in everyday life. Building on this basic knowledge, students will learn about the role that these different parts of the brain play in helping us manage stress. Students will also participate in small-group and whole-class discussions about the role of stress in their lives.

Objectives: Students will identify basic functions of the "upstairs" and "downstairs" parts of the brain. Students will identify sources of stress at school and outside of school, and will identify various ways they currently manage stress in their daily lives.

Time: 45–60 minutes (Grades 3–8)
Materials:

   Video links: Upstairs/Downstairs Brain videos (Dan Siegel, Jeanette Yoffe)
   Infographic: Upstairs vs Downstairs Brain (see page 30)
   T-Chart: Sources of Stress (see page 31)
   Small Group Activity: Stress and the Brain (see page 32)
   Markers/chart paper
   Pencils/notebook paper

Background Information for the Teacher

This lesson focuses on two concepts: 1) the function of two parts of the brain, and 2) the effects of stress in everyday life. There is a lot of student-friendly information about the upstairs and downstairs brain. You can search YouTube for short video explanations, such as this adult-level explanation by Daniel Siegel (www.youtube.com/watch?v=qFTljLo1bK8) or this student-friendly version by Jeanette Yoffe (www.youtube.com/watch?v=H_dxnYhdyuY). For a clear explanation, read *The Whole Brain Child* (Siegel & Bryson, 2011). This parenting book and its accompanying workbook have great application for anybody working with youth; they have examples, clear explanations, and recommendations for how to notice and respond appropriately when students are not accessing their "upstairs brain" skillfully.

The American Psychological Association (APA) surveys thousands of Americans about stress. The most recent report includes information on sources of stress for adults and children. Interestingly, in 2017, 8–12-year-olds and 13–17-year-olds reported the same sources of stress: (1) doing well in school, (2) getting along with friends, (3) worrying if their family had enough money, and (4) thinking about how they look. Doing research on current sources and effects of stress can help make the concepts in this chapter more relevant and timely for your students.

Lesson 1: Introduction to Stress and the Brain

Step 1—Activate Background Knowledge

Ask students what they already know about the mind and/or brain. Accept any responses, and do not feel compelled to engage in any lengthy discussion about their responses. This warm-up activity is to activate any prior knowledge students may already have related to the brain and its functions.

Step 2—Introduce New Concepts

Introduce the concepts of "Upstairs Brain" and "Downstairs Brain"

1. Show students the *Upstairs vs Downstairs Brain* infographic and describe the role each part of the brain serves in keeping us healthy and safe. Refer to "Background Information for the Teacher" to familiarize yourself with the basic functions of these two parts of the brain.
    a. Downstairs Brain (a.k.a, reptilian brain because it is the oldest part of our brain). You could say, "*It works like a watchdog, keeping constant guard to ensure we stay safe. If you saw a snake on a hiking trail, the downstairs brain would send a quick message to your body that there is danger and you need to get away from it. Without thinking, your body would react. Your heart might beat faster, your breathing might become more rapid, and your muscles would spring into action so you could get away as fast as possible. This part of our brain helps us react quickly to keep us out of danger. This part of the brain controls our basic bodily functions such as breathing, heartbeat, digestion, and blood pressure.*"
    b. Upstairs Brain (a.k.a. mammalian brain because it is the newest part of our brain and only mammals have this part; properly called the pre-frontal cortex). You could say, "*This part of our brain is responsible for helping us make decisions, remember information, organize information, plan ahead, and understand ourselves.*"
2. Then, explain how our minds tend to overuse the downstairs brain when we feel stressed and how that can limit access to the upstairs brain. You could say, "*Our brain has different parts that have different jobs to help us stay safe and healthy. The bottom part of our brain or downstairs brain is like the watchdog that is always looking out for us, trying to keep us safe. It is responsible for our "fight/flight/freeze" response. When we get startled, it tells our bodies to jump, or run, or freeze in place. This is a very important part of our brain, but often times, it thinks we are in danger, when we really are not. The downstairs brain is trying to do its best to keep you safe, and it is our job to help communicate with this part of our brain and let*

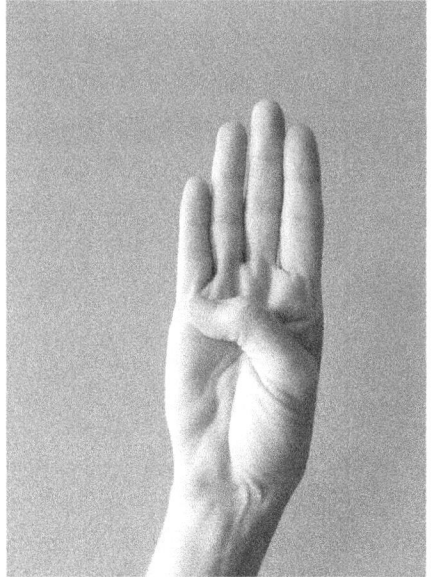

(Thumb=Downstairs Brain)   (Folded fingers=Upstairs Brain)

Figure 2.1   A Handy Model of the Brain

it know we are okay. We can do this with our breath. If I get scared, and my heart beats rapidly, I can take a few slow deep breaths to help calm my downstairs brain and my body.

The upstairs brain is this top/front part of our brain. It is in charge of helping us plan, make good decisions, get along with our classmates, focus and take tests, and learn new things. At school, we need to use the upstairs brain all the time! The problem is, if the downstairs brain feels like we are not safe, it can make it very hard for us to use the upstairs part of our brain. However, if we can do things to keep our downstairs brain calm, we can use the upstairs brain.

Introduce the concept of "flipping one's lid"

This is when the downstairs brain reacts and limits our access to the upstairs/thinking part of our brain); discuss how it can help to understand what is happening in the brain when this occurs. (In preparation, search Google for "upstairs/downstairs brain explanation" or watch the Dan Siegel video to hear it explained in adult- and student-friendly terms.)

Say, *"We can also learn ways to control this stress response so that we feel more in control, calmer and more focused throughout the day."*

Introduce the term "stress" and discuss its definition(s)

Typically, the conversation will focus on negative stress. Come up with a student-friendly definition (as a class) that helps the students understand and remember what "stress" is. Students can describe times when they have felt "stressed" or talk about a time their parent or someone they know said they were "stressed." Ultimately, a group definition should include the idea that stress arises when we feel like we do not have the resources to match the demands of the situation. This can be a very uncomfortable feeling for children because they lack the ability to control or change unpleasant situations.

Say, *"Based on our discussion, it sounds like stress is when you have too much to do and you don't have enough time; stress is when you feel bad because you can't get everything done; stress is when something unpleasant is happening but feel like you don't have any control over the situation or you can't make it stop. Later we will talk more about the effect of stress on our minds and bodies. Today, let's think about sources of stress at school and at home."*

Depending on the students' writing skills, you may decide to have small groups or individual students complete the Sources of Stress T-Chart for stressors at home and school. Pass out the T-Chart or have them make their own T-Chart on a piece of paper.

Give students 3–5 minutes to jot down a few ideas about what can be stressful at home or school. Circulate around the room as students write down their ideas. If a student is confused or cannot think of anything, you can ask probing questions to help them identify stressors.

Say, *"Is there anything that makes you nervous or tense at school? Grades? Relationships? Do you have brothers or sisters? Do you get along with them? Do you get nervous about big assignments or tests?"*

After students have the opportunity to get their ideas on paper, provide time for them to complete the Small Group Activity sheet. This is an important community-building exercise and can help students learn that their peers may have similar experiences. Provide ample time for small groups to share and discuss their feelings for the following questions on the Small Group Activity Sheet:

Table 2.1 Sample T-Chart for Small Group Activity

Stress at School	Stress at Home

- Have you ever "flipped your lid" or watched someone else "flip their lid"? What did you notice? Was it a good feeling or a bad feeling? Discuss with your group.
- In your group, brainstorm about some of the things that cause you stress. Think about home and school.
- As a group, discuss any similarities or differences you notice in your lists. Which setting (home or school) category has more sources of stress for different people in your group?
- Do you notice any patterns or surprises about the stressors you have listed?
- How do you currently deal with stress? How do you help yourself feel better?

Step 3—Discuss

Discuss the students' responses to the prompts as a class. You can write ideas on the board to summarize the group's input. After compiling the list, acknowledge that most students in the world today have many stressors that affect them daily. This can help normalize the experience of feeling stressed. It is a common feeling among youth their age.

Have students share ways they deal with stress. You might give one or two examples such as *listening to music*, or *going for a walk*. Discuss as a class and write the ideas on the board or poster paper. After the students share their ideas, note the things that require money, people to take them somewhere, etc. You may also find that students identify unhealthy coping strategies such as eating junk food or yelling at someone. It is important to honor all of the ideas shared, but you may also note that sometimes we use strategies that are not very helpful or can get us into trouble or negatively affect our health.

*Note: Some students may feel bogged down after this activity so it is important to acknowledge that although students have much on their minds, we have tools to manage the way we think about and deal with our lives, and that is why they will be learning the mindfulness practices.

IMPORTANT: Encourage students to notice that all the stressors (or nearly all) are things that have already happened or have not happened yet. You might even have them categorize the stressors on their T-Chart with this in mind.

Say, *"And if we pay attention to what is happening RIGHT NOW, those stressors are not occurring. This is the rationale for learning the* Mynd Time *strategies. These mindfulness practices allow us to focus our attention on the present moment, where stressors are NOT actually happening. When we let our brains focus on just one thing, we can give our minds a much-needed break from thinking about all the things that already happened and things that have not happened yet. And, if we are able to focus on what is occurring right now, we are better able to handle whatever happens in our lives."*

Say, *"In the next few weeks, you will be learning some strategies to manage stress at home and school. The strategies do not require money, or going to a particular location. They do not require an adult to help. They are free, useful anytime, anywhere. And, unlike some of our current coping strategies, these practices are healthy, skillful ways to attend to and manage the stress in our lives."*

Step 4—Practice
There is no formal practice in the introductory lesson but you can assure students that they will be learning and practicing useful strategies for managing stress in the days and weeks to come.

Step 5—Generalize
Conclude the lesson. It is very powerful for students to have strategies they can employ when needed without having to rely on others. These strategies can be used at school, home, in the community, wherever.

Say, *"When we are able to appropriately manage stress and feel comfortable with our own minds and bodies, we are more likely to have positive relationships with friends and family, more likely to live longer, do better in school, feel happier, etc. You will feel more powerful and in control when you have methods for helping yourself manage stress. In the coming weeks, we will learn multiple ways we can manage stress that can be done anytime, anywhere."*

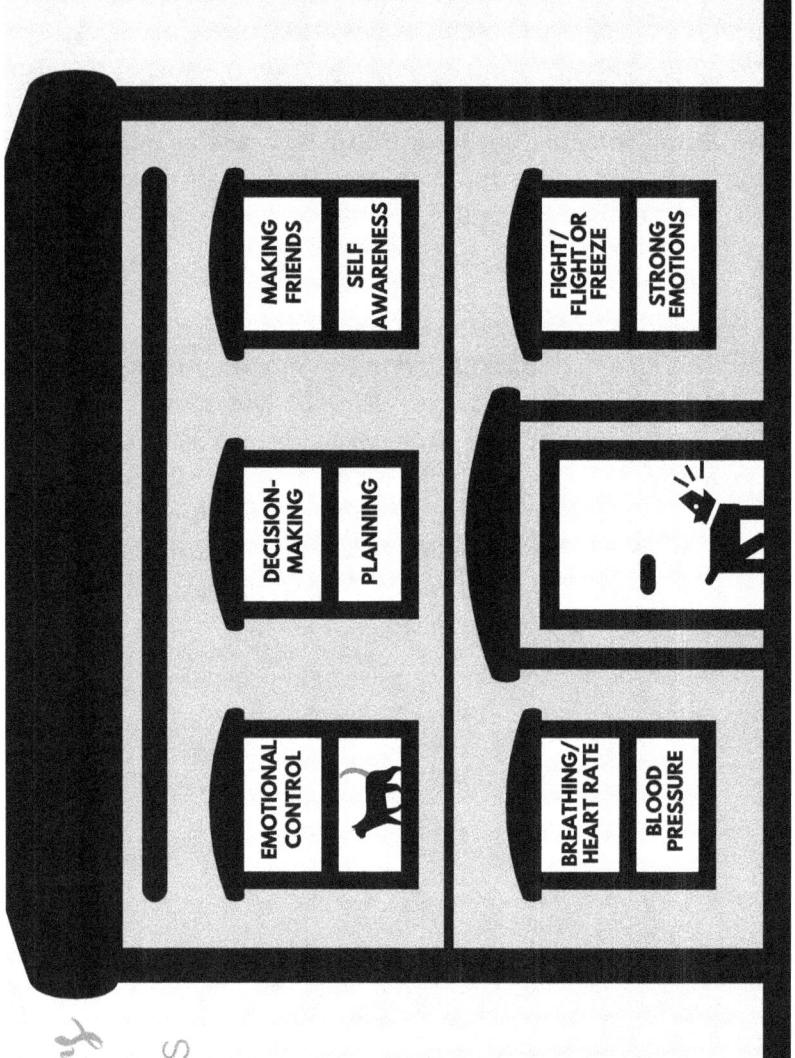

SOURCES OF STRESS
T-CHART

HOME	SCHOOL

STRESS AND THE BRAIN
SMALL GROUP ACTIVITY

Have you ever "flipped your lid" or witnessed someone else "flip their lid"? What did you notice? Was it a good feeling or a bad feeling? Discuss with your group.

In your group, brainstorm some of the things in your life that cause you stress. Think about home and school.

As a group, discuss any similarities or differences you notice in your lists. Which setting (home or school) has more sources of stress for different members of your group?

Do you notice any patterns or surprises about the stressors you have listed?

How do you currently deal with stress? How do you help yourself feel better?

© 2019 Taylor & Francis

Chapter 3

Breath Awareness

Chapter at a Glance

Lesson Overview: In this lesson, students will learn that bringing awareness to their own breathing is a vital aspect of their well-being. Considering their background knowledge of the parts of the brain, students will participate in small-group and whole-class discussions about the importance and benefits of focusing on one's breath.

Objectives: Students will describe why the breath is important and will practice the Breath Awareness strategy

Time: 45 minutes (Grades 3–5), 45+ minutes if additional writing is included (Grades 6–8)

Materials:

Script: Breath Awareness Practice (see page 38)
Infographic: Benefits of Deep Breathing (see page 39)
Small Group Activity: Breath Awareness (see page 40)
Breath Awareness Certificate (see page 41)
Chart paper/markers
Pencils/notebook paper

Background Information for the Teacher

This lesson provides instruction on two key concepts: (1) the function of the breath, and how we can regulate our breathing to respond wisely to external demands, and (2) the formal practice of breath awareness. We often take for granted the fact that our bodies do many things automatically (e.g., digestion, heartbeat, breathing), without us having to think about it. This lesson teaches students that it can actually be better for our mental and physical health to notice the quality of our breathing by attending to the rate, depth, and other physical sensations associated with our breath. There are information and resources listed in Table 3.1 about the benefits of deep breathing and attending to the breath, in general.

This is the first lesson that includes a formal mindfulness practice. Some instruction should be given on how to sit in an upright but not rigid posture, closing the eyes if that feels comfortable. (NB: Remember, closing the eyes is *not* required, and is not necessary to benefit from the formal practices.) The instruction is to focus on the physical sensations of breathing while noticing that the mind's natural tendency is to keep thinking and staying active. In this first lesson regarding formal practice, it is important to address the notion that

Table 3.1 Benefits of Deep Breathing

Benefits of Deep Breathing	Explanation
Strengthens the immune system	Provides more oxygen to your blood and can help your body metabolize nutrients
Improves the nervous system	Provides more oxygen to your brain and spinal cord to keep it healthy
Elevates mood	Deep breathing helps pump endorphins into your system which can have a positive effect on your mood
Boosts energy and stamina	Deep breathing can slow the heart rate and increase circulation that can improve energy and stamina
Relieves pain	People tend to hold their breath and tighten their muscles when they feel pain. Taking deep breaths when you are in pain works to help relax your body and can sometimes make pain subside
Increases clarity and focus	Provides oxygen to your brain and can help calm your mind so that you can concentrate and focus
Releases muscle tension	Deep breaths can help relax the muscles in your body when you are nervous, angry or scared. Usually when we feel these emotions, we have shallow breathing. If you can breathe slowly and deeply, you can help your body relax instead of constrict

there is not one "right way" to do any of these mindfulness practices. Each person has different experiences, thoughts, feelings, and physical sensations.

This is a good time to remind students that there can be some misconceptions about mindfulness, as often people associate mindfulness with relaxation. Yes, students may feel relaxed after the formal practice, but that is not a requirement or even an indicator of "successful" practice. The purpose of these practices is to bring a gentle and kind awareness to whatever is occurring in the present moment; good, bad, or neutral. This may mean that a student is more aware of discomfort or boredom, and yet another student may feel peaceful and at ease. All experiences are valid, and students need to know that their experience is acknowledged and valued.

Lesson 2: Focus on Breath Awareness

Step 1—Activate Background Knowledge
Review information covered in the Introduction lessons (downstairs/upstairs brain, stress, etc.).

Step 2—Introduce New Concept
Ask, "*What are some things our bodies need to survive?*" (Example answers are: food, water, heartbeat, oxygen/breathing, shelter.)

Explain the importance of breathing in our daily lives and that our body often regulates our breath for us.

Say, "*Our breath is something we can use to help us focus, calm down, run faster, etc. Today we will look at the benefits of good deep breathing and how we can change our breathing to help us regulate our bodies and minds.*"

Introduce the concept that our breathing changes throughout the day depending on different activities we do. Refer to information in the Small Group Activity Sheet at the end of the lesson to guide group discussion and compile responses. Discuss the fact that most of us do not take full, deep breaths, and so spend a lot of our time breathing in a shallow way that only uses the top part of our lungs. There are times when we need to breathe more quickly, and other times we need to breathe more slowly.

Say, "*Let's brainstorm ways that our breathing changes with different activities or circumstances. If we can bring our awareness to our breathing, and start to take slower, deeper breaths, we can make sure our bodies get enough oxygen during active times. And, we can also recognize how our breathing might change and become quicker and shallower when we are stressed or sad or angry, and choose to bring awareness to our breath and deepen or just allow our breath to be as it is.*"

Step 3—Discuss
We can also focus on our breathing and what it feels like in our bodies as a way to calm ourselves when we feel stressed.

Say, "*Let's talk about where we feel our breath in our bodies (examples: nostrils, top lip, throat, chest, stomach). When we focus our attention on where we most feel our breath, we can give our minds a break from all the thinking and feeling we do throughout the day. When your mind gets a break, you might feel more refreshed, calmer, maybe more energized, happier, etc. And, by attending to the physical sensations of breathing, we can become more familiar with our own breathing.*"

Step 4—Practice
Say, "*Let's practice Strategy #1: Breath Awareness.*"

Use the script verbatim, modify it to fit your own voice/word choice, or play the audio recording.

Step 5—Generalize
Say, *"We will practice this strategy each day in class for a while. You can also practice bringing your awareness to your breath throughout the school day and at home. Maybe when you are standing in line after P.E., you notice your breathing is faster because you just ran and played. Or, you may notice your breathing right before you fall asleep at night. Remember, we are not necessarily trying to change our breathing, but when you notice what your breathing is like, it might naturally deepen or slow down. If it doesn't, just notice what it feels like. See what happens when you do that."*

Script for Breath Awareness Practice

Find a comfortable seated position, feet on the floor, back is straight, shoulders are relaxed. Allow the eyes to close gently, if that feels okay, or just lower your gaze.
(Pause)
Checking in with the sensations of your body, beginning to bring your awareness to your breath and where you feel your breath in your body.
(Pause)
It may be helpful to take a few slow, deep breaths, to help you notice the sensation of breathing in your body. Maybe you feel the air moving in and out through your nose or throat. You may feel the physical sensation as your lungs fill with air as you breathe in and release as you breath out. Maybe you sense movement in your stomach as you breath in and out. Notice each cycle of breathing as you inhale and exhale.
(Pause for 30 seconds)
Notice each breath as it comes and goes. Allowing the body to release any tension that is not needed.
(Long Pause: 1 minute)
If you notice that your mind has wandered away from the sensations of breathing you may choose to gently bring your awareness back to the breath, back to the sensations in the body as you inhale and exhale.
(Pause)
Breathing in, breathing out, allowing you this time right here, right now, to just be. Just noticing the sensations of the breath in the body.
(Pause)
You may take a few nice deep breaths, inhaling and exhaling deeply. Bring your awareness back into this room.
(Ring bell)

When you are ready you may slowly open your eyes.
Remember, that giving your mind a few minutes to focus on just one thing, like your breath, can give your brain a welcomed break. As you go through your day, see if you can notice your breathing and what it feels like during different times of the day or night. When you are standing in line at lunch, waiting for the bus, running at recess, doing your homework, or going to sleep. See if you can find a few moments to rest between thoughts and just feel your breath in your body. Enjoy the rest of your day.

Benefits of *Deep Breathing!*

- Helps with Digestion
- Increases Energy
- Relieves headaches
- Improves Sleep
- Improves perfomance

© 2019 Taylor & Francis

**BREATH AWARENESS
SMALL GROUP ACTIVITY**

List times of the day or activities when your breathing is slow and deep.

List times of the day or activities when your breathing is fast and shallow.

Why do you think your breath changes with different activities?

When you feel stressed, what is your breathing like?

© 2019 Taylor & Francis

This certificate is awarded to

_____

in recognition of
PRACTICING BREATH AWARENESS

"If you are breathing, there is more right with you than wrong."
- Jon Kabat-Zinn

_____   _____
Signature   Date

© 2019 Taylor & Francis

Chapter 4

Body Awareness

Chapter at a Glance

Lesson Overview: In this lesson, students will learn that their minds and bodies communicate regularly and can provide helpful information about our well-being. Activating their background knowledge of stress and breath awareness, students will participate in small-group and whole-class discussions about the importance and benefits of attending to physical sensations in the body as a mechanism for regulating stress. Students will practice the Body Scan.

Objective: Students will be able to explain the connection between stress, emotional states and the physical body. They will also be able to describe why body awareness is important to the upstairs and downstairs brain working together.

Time: 30 minutes (Grades 3–5), 45 minutes (Grades 6–8)

Materials:

Script: Body Awareness Practice (Body Scan) (see page 47)
Infographic: How Stress Affects the Body (see page 49)
T-Chart: Stress and the Body (see page 50)
Body Awareness Certificate (see page 51)
Chart paper/markers
Pencils/notebook paper

Background Information for the Teacher

This lesson builds on the knowledge and practice with breath awareness in the previous lesson. It is important for students to have ample time to experience the breath awareness practice so that they have a familiarity with sitting in an upright posture, settling the mind and body, and learning to focus the attention. After a few weeks of the breath awareness practice, students are ready to learn the concept of how stress affects the mind/body and the body scan practice.

Awareness of physical body sensations is an important skill to develop for many reasons. On a purely physical level, our bodies provide a great deal of information about our health, energy levels, pain or injuries, and if we feel hungry or full. Many people ignore the messages their bodies send them regarding their own physical health. The body scan practice provides students with the formal practice of attending to sensations that can be pleasant, unpleasant or even neutral or numb. The purpose of the body scan is not to try to feel anything in particular, but rather notice how the body feels in the present moment, during the practice. In addition to information about our physical bodies, the sensations in the body can also communicate information about our emotional states. If you are someone who has experienced anxiety, you may be familiar with physical sensations that accompany that emotional state (tightness in the chest, rapid heartbeat, etc.).

This lesson allows students to explore the messages their bodies provide when they feel stressed or overwhelmed. In addition to the physical sensations, this lesson also explores the thoughts and feelings that accompany the physical sensations when they feel stressed. For example, a student might feel tightness in their stomach when they have to stand in front of the school for a musical performance, and their mind may be racing with thoughts such as, "I am scared. What if everybody laughs at me? What if I make a mistake?" The body scan practice allows students to become familiar with the physical sensations in their own bodies, as well as discover the types of thoughts and feelings occur during times when they feel stressed.

It is common for people to ignore or suppress physical sensations that accompany stress. The body scan practice invites students to do the opposite: turn toward, rather than away from the physical sensations in the body, and acknowledge the nature of the thoughts and feelings that arise during stressful times. This formal practice is the starting point for bringing awareness to habitual patterns and responses. If students are able to notice how they respond habitually or without thinking, it is possible to learn new ways of relating and responding to stressful events in their lives.

Lesson 3: Body Awareness

Step 1—Activate Background Knowledge
Review the purpose of the breath awareness practice and get students feedback about what went well, what they liked, or did not like. Field any questions/comments: "Am I doing it correctly?", "I still think about other stuff when I'm supposed to focus on my breath", "I don't like sitting still", "Why do we have to do this?", etc. (Note: Remember that a wide range of experiences is expected and completely normal. There is no need to try to convince students to enjoy the practices. The purpose of mindfulness is to be aware of what is occurring: pleasant, unpleasant or neutral.)

Step 2—Introduce New Concept
Introduce the idea that when our lives are stressful, this can affect our minds and bodies and general health.

Say, *"Think about times when you were feeling upset or stressed. How did this affect you? Maybe it was hard to concentrate. Sometimes people have headaches when they feel stressed. In your small groups, discuss how stress affects your thinking mind and your body. We will share our ideas as a whole group."*

Compile the small groups' ideas on a T-Chart of how stress affects the mind and body. Students can draw the T-Chart below or use the template on page 50.

Step 3—Discuss
Say: *"So now that we see how stress affects our minds and bodies, what do you think would happen if we could manage to keep our stress low? There is a lot of research that says if you can manage stress, you will live longer, get better grades, have better friendships, and enjoy your life more! How might we move away from all the thinking, thinking, thinking and help our downstairs brain feel safe?"*

You could refer back to the downstairs/upstairs brain infographic to show where basic bodily functions are managed in the brain, to show that if we want to help that "watchdog" part of our brain calm down, we need to pay attention to the signals our downstairs brain gives us in our bodies.

Table 4.1 T-Chart for Group Activity: Effects of stress on the mind and body

Effects of Stress on YOUR MIND	Effects of Stress on YOUR BODY

Say: *"Turning toward how we feel physically (in our bodies) helps give our minds a break and it lets our downstairs brain know that we are okay."*

You could provide some examples of how the thinking mind actually perpetuates or makes stress worse through the thoughts we think. (Possible examples: *nervous* during spelling bee, *mad* at friend/parent/sibling, *disappointed/frustrated* with video game, got bad grade on test, etc.)

Say, *"If we attend to what we are feeling right now in our bodies, we can sometimes quiet those unhelpful thoughts and drop into the present moment experience. Often times, what is physically happening in our bodies is not nearly as bad as the thoughts and feelings we have about those physical sensations."*

Step 4—Practice

Say, *"Let's practice Strategy #2: Body Scan."*

Use the script verbatim or modify it to fit your own voice/word choice or play the audio recording. Depending on your classroom setting, the body scan can be done in a seated position or lying down. (Note: If you have students lie down, communicate ground rules such as: stay in your own space; your body needs to be still; eyes closed or looking straight up at the ceiling; be respectful of your neighbors by not making any noise. Expect some movement and possibly some sleeping. As students become more accustomed to being still, they will get better at sustaining a posture (either seated or lying down) with minimal movement.)

Step 5—Generalize

Say, *"It's important to be aware of how your body feels, not just when you feel bad or stressed, but throughout the day. At first, it may be difficult to bring your attention to different parts of your body, but with practice, you will become more sensitive to what your body is telling you. When we are more connected to our bodies, we can respond appropriately to the cues it gives us and live healthy lives."*

Script for Body Awareness Practice (The Body Scan)

During the body scan we will scan through the entire body, starting with the feet and working our way up to the head. Find a comfortable, dignified posture, closing your eyes or lowering your gaze to turn your focus inward.

During this practice, you do not need to move each part of your body, or try to change anything you are feeling. Just see what you feel as we scan the body. There may be areas in the body where you do not feel anything and that is normal. Just check into those areas each time as if you feel something. You may feel pleasant or unpleasant sensations, or you may feel numbness in parts of your body. Whatever sensations you feel in your body are just fine.

Starting with the feet. Bring your awareness to your feet. Do you feel your socks or shoes against your feet? Can you feel the pressure of the ground pressing against the bottom of your feet? See if you can sense your toes and the tops of your feet—or not. Your heels and ankles, what is here to feel? Just notice any sensations or lack of sensation in the feet.

(Pause)

Shifting your attention to your lower legs. Do you feel your clothing against your skin? Can you feel the bend in your knees just by sensing this inside your body?

(Pause)

Bringing awareness to your upper legs and hips. Can you feel where your legs and the chair meet? If you notice places where you may be holding tension, you may invite your body to release. If you can't, just be aware of how your body feels.

(Pause)

Shift your focus to your torso: your back and stomach, rib cage and chest. Can you feel your body moving as you breathe? What about your heart? Can you feel it beating? Maybe you can feel your lungs expand and contract as you breathe.

(Pause)

Moving to the middle of your back and up through your shoulder blades. Do you feel your chair or clothes touching your back? Maybe you notice warm or cool sensations, or the texture of clothing, or even different types of sensations in your body: pulsing, movement, numbness. What is here to be felt?

(Pause)

Move your attention to your upper back and shoulders; continue shifting your focus to your arms and out to your hands. You may notice that you feel the position of your hands without having to look at them. Maybe you can feel the desk under your hands, or your own two hands touching.

(Pause)

Sense your wrists, lower arms, elbows, and upper arms. Are your arms touching your sides, your legs, or your desk? Just sense the physical feelings in your arms right now in this moment.

(Pause)

Shift your attention to your shoulders and neck, moving your attention upward; sense your jawbone and mouth.

(Pause)

Notice your tongue, your teeth, and throat.

(Pause)

Moving up, feel your cheeks and nose.

(Pause)

Bring awareness to your eyes in their sockets, your forehead and temples. Inviting all the muscles and bones in your face to release any tension or tightness if that feels right.

(Pause)

Now opening awareness to include your entire body, allowing all sensations in the body to be just as they are in this moment.

(Pause)

Taking a moment to be grateful for this body, with all 206 bones and over 600 muscles working together to keep your body strong and healthy. Take a few deep breaths and when you are ready, you may open your eyes. Take time throughout the day to notice what your body feels like when you feel calm and relaxed, excited, angry, nervous, etc. If you become familiar with what your body feels like when it is resting or calm, you will be better able to respond when your body sends messages when you are stressed. Try doing the body scan at different times: riding in the car, right when you wake up in the morning, after recess or other activities. What happens when you listen and respond to what your body is telling you?

Enjoy the rest of your day!

How Stress Affects THE BODY

DIGESTION
UPSET STOMACH, DIGESTIVE DISORDERS, STOMACH PAIN

HEAD/BRAIN
HEADACHES, DIZZINESS, ANXIETY, PANIC ATTACKS, CHRONIC FATIGUE

HEART
INCREASED HEART RATE, STROKES, HEART DISEASE

MUSCLES
MUSCLE TENSION, GRINDING TEETH, CLENCHED JAW

Stress Facts:

39% — MILLENNIALS WHO REPORT THEIR STRESS HAS INCREASED

69% — AMERICANS REPORTING PHYSICAL SYMPTOMS ASSOCIATED WITH STRESS

We cannot eliminate stress from our lives, but we can learn to manage how we respond to it.

© 2019 Taylor & Francis

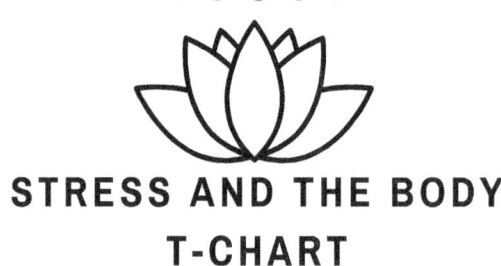

STRESS AND THE BODY
T-CHART

Effects of Stress on YOUR MIND	Effects of Stress on YOUR BODY

© 2019 Taylor & Francis

eRESOURCES

MYND TIME

This certificate is awarded to

_____

in recognition of

PRACTICING BODY AWARENESS

"To listen to your body and respect how it feels
is a powerful act of self-love."
- **Sonia Choquette**

_____ _____
Signature   Date

© 2019 Taylor & Francis

Chapter 5

Focus on Gratitude

Chapter at a Glance

Lesson Overview: In this lesson, students will learn that they can build the skill of being grateful. Activating their background knowledge about the effects of stress on the mind and body, students will learn about the positive effect gratitude has on the mind and body. They will list people, places, and objects they are grateful for as a mechanism for regulating stress. Students will learn the formal practice of Focus on Gratitude.

Objective: Students will describe how being grateful can improve one's mood, perspective and overall well-being.

Time: 25 minutes (Grades 3–5), 35 minutes (Grades 6–8)

Materials:

Script: Gratitude Practice (see page 57)
Infographic: What Good is Gratitude? (see page 58)
Gratitude Practice Certificate (see page 59)
Chart paper/markers
Pencils/notebook paper

Background Information for the Teacher

In this lesson, students will learn that it is possible to change your thinking and mood by focusing on people, places, and things that you are grateful for. Often students believe that life happens to them and that they have no control over how they think or respond to stressful situations. This lesson teaches students to focus intentionally on feeling grateful as a way to formally practice changing one's thoughts.

The human brain naturally focuses on the negative aspects of our experiences. This is called the Negativity Bias. Dr. Rick Hanson provides a great description of this natural inclination of the brain in his book, *Buddha's Brain* (2009). He also has a blog that covers topics ranging from dealing with difficult emotions, to creating more joy, and even contains quizzes for you to reflect on your own life (see www.rickhanson.net/blog).

Dating back to caveman days when our survival depended on avoiding danger, it makes sense that our brains hyper-focused on any potential harm or danger. Fast forward to today, we have that same part of our brain, but are not frequently in life or death situations where we have to scan the environment for hungry tigers or bears. However, our brains are still on high alert to other modern-day threats to our well-being, like making a speech in front of the class, confronting an angry friend, earning a bad grade on a test, or losing a championship game. These "threats" to our well-being activates that same response in our downstairs brain that tells our mind and body that we are not safe. It is important for students to understand how the human brain works in its default mode, but also understand that as human beings, we have the capacity to override, or at least choose how to respond to, the information our brain receives. By attending to how the brain reacts to perceived threats, the mind can begin to deal with the real or perceived threats more calmly and effectively.

There is a great deal of recent research on the positive effects of mindfulness which can greatly increase your background knowledge for this lesson, as well as the next lesson and practice on Kindness toward Self and Others. Now more than ever, neuroscience is providing scientific evidence of what were previously anecdotal reports. Through brain scans and other cutting edge technology, scientists are learning more and more about the different parts of the brain and the potential positive effects of mindfulness practices on the various functions of the brain. The American Mindfulness Research Association (AMRA) has a website dedicated to sharing mindfulness research. David Black authored a chapter in the *Handbook on Mindfulness: Theory, Research and Practice* that reviews the state of research on mindfulness training for youth (2015).

Lesson 4: Focus on Gratitude

Step 1—Activate Background Knowledge
Review the body scan lesson and discuss any questions or comments students have about the body scan practice.

Step 2—Introduce New Concepts

Focus on Gratitude
Introduce the new concept and practice: Focus on Gratitude. Share some of the facts from the list or the Gratitude Infographic below to help students understand the rationale for strategy. Here are a few other fun facts about the positive effects of gratitude.

1. One study showed that people who wrote down what they were grateful for each day were in better health and felt happier than people who just wrote down daily events or neutral things.
2. People who say thank you, or tell someone they are grateful for them, have an increase in "happy effects" and a decrease in depressive symptoms.
3. One researcher implemented a gratitude curriculum for children aged 8–11 years old; these students had more appreciation and positive emotions than the students who did not receive the lessons.
4. Gratitude has been shown to have a positive impact on teenagers' behavior, GPA, and higher levels of general happiness.
5. Gratitude can help you manage stress better.
6. If you haven't been very grateful, you can start now. Gratitude is an attitude you can learn and practice.

Negativity Bias
Introduce the natural tendency for the human brain to focus more on negative events and thoughts. Discuss why this is (survival/fight/flight response). Be sure to reiterate that it is not something to feel bad about, but rather understand and work with this natural propensity of the downstairs brain.

Say, "*When we understand that our brain has this habit, we can work to acknowledge it, and even shift the focus to more positive thoughts, events, etc. One way we can shift our awareness is to intentionally think about things we are grateful to have in our lives.*"

Ask students take 3 minutes to write down everything they are grateful for. This can be material possessions, people, pets, places, etc. There is no need to shape or limit what students write down during this exercise.

If individual students struggle, you can offer a few suggestions, but really this is a time for students to determine what they are grateful for. Some students have very challenging lives and may not feel grateful for their family, home, belongings, etc. If students have a hard time identifying things on a personal level, you might encourage them to consider less personal things to be grateful for (e.g. safe school to attend, Play Station or phone, clean water to drink, etc.) The purpose of this practice is to cultivate a sense of gratitude. The actual people, places or objects students choose are less important.

Step 3—Discuss
Have students share what they wrote and honor what they share. The act of sharing one's ideas with the group is a way to build community and connection. As the teacher, you can provide a positive example of respecting diverse views and experiences by allowing students to express themselves in these types of small-group/whole-class discussions. Students can learn a great deal about their peers and find connections or commonalities with people they would not ordinarily talk to. Acknowledge that each of us has things to be grateful for, and we can choose to focus our attention on gratitude rather than wait until something good happens.

Step 4—Practice
Say, *"Let's practice Strategy #3: Gratitude Practice."*

Use the script verbatim, modify it to fit your own voice/word choice, or play the audio recording.

Step 5—Generalize
Say, *"When you focus on one or more things that you are grateful for, you are setting yourself up to feel happier and more connected to your life."*

Script for Gratitude Practice

Sit in a comfortable seated, upright position. Close your eyes or lower your gaze. Bring your awareness to your breath, and take a few moments to settle into this moment, right here, right now.

(Pause for 30 seconds)

Turning your attention toward people, places or things you are grateful for. You might picture someone or something in particular that you are grateful for. Really focus on the feeling you feel inside when you think about being grateful for this person or pet or object. You can bring to mind what you appreciate about this person. Are they kind, helpful, funny? Do they take care of you? Maybe you can remember a specific time or place. Or, you may simply feel a general sense of gratitude for having this person, pet or object in your life.

(Pause for 1 minute)

Continue to focus on just one person or thing, or you may choose to think about other people, places and things you are grateful for. Just take a few moments to focus on who or what you are truly thankful for in your life. You can focus on just one thing, or more than one thing. The purpose of this practice is to cultivate the feeling of gratitude in your mind, body and heart.

(Pause for 30 seconds)

If you find yourself lost in thought or thinking about something else, you can notice this and begin again with your focus on gratitude, bringing to mind a person or pet, a special place or object that you appreciate in your life.

(Pause for 1 minute)

Take a few nice slow deep breaths, and when you are ready, slowly open your eyes. Bring your awareness back to your surroundings, back into this room. Throughout your day, take a breath, pause, and think about the things you are grateful for. Remember, feeling grateful can make your mind and body feel calm and happy. Have a great day.

eRESOURCES →

Fun Facts about grateful people!

What Good is Gratitude?

Community.
GRATEFUL PEOPLE WILL HAVE A STRONG BOND TO LOCAL COMMUNITY.

PSYCHOLOGICAL.
Gratitude is related to age: For every 10 years, gratitude increases by 5%.

Youth.
13% FEWER FIGHTS.
20% MORE LIKELY TO GET GOOD GRADES.
10% LESS LIKELY TO START SMOKING.

CHARITY.
20% Grateful people on average give 20% more TIME & MONEY.

WORK.
HAPPY PEOPLE'S INCOME IS ROUGHLY 7% HIGHER.

Health.
GRATEFUL PEOPLE WILL HAVE 10% FEWER STRESS-RELATED ILLNESSES.

LIFE.
An overall positive attitude can add up to 7 years to your life.

© 2019 Taylor & Francis

MYND TIME

This certificate is awarded to

_____

in recognition of
PRACTICING GRATITUDE

"Gratitude is the healthiest of all human emotions. The more you express gratitude for what you have, the more likely you will have even more to express gratitude for."
- Zig Ziglar

_____ _____
Signature   Date

© 2019 Taylor & Francis

Chapter 6

Kindness Toward Self and Others

Chapter at a Glance

Lesson Overview: This lesson is similar in focus to the Focus on Gratitude practice. The purpose of this practice is to improve one's skill in cultivating kind wishes toward oneself and others, regardless of thoughts, feelings or external events.

Objective: Students will describe how being positive can improve one's mood, relationship with others, and overall well-being. Students will also be able to acknowledge that the desire to be happy is a common wish of all people (whether they like them or not).

Time: 25 minutes (Grades 3–5), 35 minutes (Grades 6–8)

Materials:

Script: Kindness Practice (see page 65)
Infographic: Kindness (see page 66)
Kindness Practice Certificate (see page 67)
Chart paper/markers
Pencils/notebook paper

Background Information for the Teacher

In this lesson students learn about doing something without being attached to the outcome. Like the previous lesson, students are encouraged to cultivate a state of mind that is independent of what is occurring in the lives. This means that even if you have a challenging home life or a bad day at school, you can still learn to skillfully tap into a wish for yourself and others to experience good health, safety, joy, etc.

This can be a difficult concept to grasp because most students are familiar with being happy when people respond the way they want them to or when events turn out the way they wished. We do not typically send kind thoughts to ourselves when we think we did something bad, nor do we send kind wishes to other people unless we like them. Instead of waiting for life to cooperate with our likes/dislikes, we can practice wishing for good health, safety, and joy in our own lives, and wishing that for others without being caught up in the outcome or effects of our well-wishes.

Developing the capacity to wish well for oneself and others is the foundation of compassion. When students cultivate compassion, they are able to acknowledge and respect other people's points of view, they realize that they have many things in common with their peers (regardless of liking or not liking the peer), which can support increased social connection (Kok et al., 2013), decreased bias (Kang, Gray & Dovidio, 2014), increased empathy (Klimecki, Leiberg, Lamm, and Singer, 2013). In addition to these positive effects on one's relationships with others, doing the formal Kindness Practice can also improve *self*-compassion, and develop the skill of being less critical of ourselves (Shahar et al., 2015).

Lesson 5: Focus on Kindness

Step 1—Activate Background Knowledge
Review the Focus on Gratitude lesson and formal practice. Accept feedback from students on the formal practice, any new awareness to different thoughts/feelings related to this practice. Ask students if they noticed themselves thinking more about what they are grateful for, or not.

Step 2—Introduce New Concept
Introduce the next strategy: Kindness Practice. Similar to the research on gratitude, there is a growing body of research that has found really positive emotional, physical, and social benefits to focusing on the bright side of things. Here are some fun facts you can share with students:

1. Positive/happy people live longer (7½ years longer on average).
2. Happy people don't get sick as often.
3. Happy people sleep better.
4. They feel more connected to friends and family (and not isolated/alone).
5. Positive thinking people are kinder to themselves.
6. Happy people often report a full, meaningful, purpose-driven life.
7. Happy people often have lower heart rates and lower amounts of cortisol (stress hormone) in their bodies.

Step 3—Discuss
Have students work in small groups or individually to identify things that are positive about themselves and their lives. This is very similar to the gratitude lesson but there is a slight shift toward students looking inward a bit more. Can they identify their own strengths? Can they acknowledge these things and feel good about it? If they do not feel positive about themselves, can they identify a positive characteristic that a close friend or loved one would choose?

It is reasonable to provide an example or two, but refrain from doing all the work. Students will learn to reflect on their own feelings and thoughts when they have the time and space to do so. After students have some time to brainstorm together or independently, segue into the idea that sometimes things are not the way we want them, within ourselves, or in our lives. This can be a complicated concept for students to understand. When we wish well, we are not trying to *make* it happen, but just choosing to feel and send kind thoughts to ourselves and others.

Say, *"There are things that happen that are beyond our control, but one thing we can control is our wish for joy in our own lives. We do not have to wait for everything to be perfect, or any certain way. We can wish ourselves kindness no matter what is happening. We can also send well-wishes to others, no matter what is happening. Again, we are not practicing making things happen a certain way, but rather choosing to feel kindness, on purpose, in the present moment."*

Step 4—Practice
Say, *"Let's practice Strategy #4: Kindness Practice."*

Use the script verbatim, modify it to fit your own voice/word choice, or play the audio recording.

Step 5—Generalize
Say, *"The purpose of practicing sending kind wishes to yourself and others is to increase your capacity to be kind. Kindness is a skill. We can actually improve our ability to be kind, but we have to practice. Over the next few days, see if you notice yourself thinking badly about yourself or someone else. Can you pause, and instead send yourself or that person kindness? ('May I be safe, may I be healthy, may I be happy, may I live my life with ease.') We do not have to wait for others to be kind to us; we can cultivate a sense of kindness within ourselves that does not depend on what is happening in our lives. And, when we do that, we can improve our relationships, feel better about ourselves, and feel a sense of ease, even in stressful times."*

Script for Kindness Practice Toward Self and Others

For this next strategy, you are going to send positive wishes to yourself and others. So take a moment to get comfortable in an upright seated posture, checking in with your body, relaxing if possible, and closing your eyes if that feels okay, or just lowering your gaze.

(Pause)

Begin by bringing awareness to your chest, and to your physical heart. Notice your heart beat today, right now. Just noticing what that feels like in your body, not to change anything, just to know how your heart feels right now.

(Pause)

In this practice, we work toward having a kinder, more open approach toward ourselves and others. It may feel awkward or fake when you start out, but that is okay.

Bring to mind one person you feel a connection with. This could be a family member, a friend, a teacher, or pet. Imagine this person being near you, sitting by you. You may think about why you are grateful for this person.

(Pause)

By repeating these words in your mind, send this person friendly wishes.

May you be safe. (pause, then repeat)

May you be healthy and strong. (pause, then repeat)

May you be truly happy. (pause, then repeat)

May you live your life with ease. (pause, then repeat)

(Pause)

Moving the attention from your friend to yourself. Thinking about yourself with kindness and compassion, repeating and sending the same kind wishes to yourself.

May I be safe. (pause, then repeat)

May I be healthy and strong. (pause, then repeat)

May I be truly happy. (pause, then repeat)

May I live my life with ease. (pause, then repeat)

(Pause)

Bring your awareness to your breath, gathering up these wishes for yourself. Allow yourself to feel these kind words soak into your mind and body. Safety, good health, happiness and ease. When we focus on kind thoughts and wishes, whether we are focusing on ourselves or sending these positive wishes to others, we are activating the happy part of our brain. When you feel good inside, you can share that goodness with others.

Have a great rest of your day!

 Love

Happiness

 Optimism

KINDNESS

 Friendship

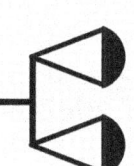 Balance

 Peace

MYND TIME

This certificate is awarded to

_____

in recognition of
PRACTICING KINDNESS

_____

"Let us fill our hearts with our own compassion- toward ourselves and all living beings."
- Thich Nhat Hanh

_____   _____
Signature   Date

© 2019 Taylor & Francis

Chapter 7

Open Awareness

Chapter at a Glance

Lesson Overview: In this lesson, students will draw on their previous experience to incorporate aspects of the four previous practices into a more fluid, open awareness practice. Now that students are comfortable with sitting for a few minutes, bringing awareness to different sensations or ideas in the present moment, they are ready to expand the focus of their attention. Open Awareness is just that—open. We can be receptive to whatever is occurring in the present moment (e.g., sounds, thoughts, feelings, bodily sensations).

Lesson Objective: Students will practice widening their attention to allow thoughts, feelings, physical sensations, and sounds to come and go in the present moment.

Time: 10 minutes (Grades 3–8)

Materials:

Script: Open Awareness Practice (see page 73)
Infographic: Open Awareness (see page 75)
Group Activity: Open Awareness (see page 76)
Open Awareness Certificate (see page 77)

Background Information for the Teacher

Rick Hanson describes the purpose of practicing open awareness thus: "The space of awareness allows every content of mind to be or not to be, to come and to go. Thoughts are just thoughts, sounds are just sounds, situations are just situations, and people are just being themselves" (2009, p. 115). This is the foundation of the concept of "equanimity." Equanimity is a state of mind that allows us to see and experience whatever is occurring in the present moment without being caught up or shaken by it. This mind state serves as the basis for finding inner joy regardless of external circumstances.

The human mind's natural tendency is to react to stimuli in our internal and external environment. We typically want more of things we find pleasant, and want to avoid or decrease things we find unpleasant. Although this is a normal habit of the mind, we can learn to disrupt this pattern of reacting with a greater capacity to bring awareness to what is occurring in the present moment without the habitual tendency to react. When we practice open awareness, we are increasing our capacity to be present with our direct life experiences, which positions us in a more healthy state of mind so that we may *choose* how we *respond*, rather than *react* hastily and carelessly.

To experience the open awareness practice before teaching it, go to Tara Brach's website (www.tarabrach.com) and listen to a number of 15–20-minute guided meditations on open awareness. For a shorter version (6 minutes), search for Elisha Goldstein's Sky of Awareness on YouTube (www.youtube.com).

Lesson 6: Open Awareness

Step 1—Activate Background Knowledge
Ask students about the four practices they have already learned. Which do they prefer? Have they found any of the practices useful outside of school? Have they noticed any changes in the way they respond to stress in their lives? Field questions and comments as needed.

Step 2—Introduce New Concept
Say, *"Each of the practices we have learned over the past few weeks/months have all invited us to focus our attention in a narrow and particular way. Sometimes we focus on the physical sensations of breathing with our Breath Awareness practice, sometimes the other sensations in our body with the Body Scan, or we focused on particular ways of feeling like when we learned the Gratitude and Kindness practices,. In this next practice, we will take what we have learned from the other practices to see how we can open our attention more widely and actually allow ourselves to notice all of the things occurring in the present moment: physical sensations, thoughts and feelings, even sounds in the environment."*

You might describe the previous practices as having a laser-beam focus, and this practice as actually widening the focus similar to an adjustable flashlight (i.e., when you adjust the focus you can make the light beam narrow and targeted, or wider and softer).

Say, *"This open awareness practice still has us practice bringing awareness to what is actually occurring in the present moment, but we can notice what is happening through our five senses, and by noticing our thoughts and feelings as they come and go. Often times, open awareness compares the mind to the sky. The sky is vast, transparent, and does not change even when conditions in the sky change. There can be storm clouds, light and fluffy clouds, or even no clouds, but the sky remains. The same can occur in our minds. Our minds can be aware of the changing conditions: sounds, physical sensations, feelings, thoughts, etc. These will come and go, just like clouds in the sky. The practice of open awareness is to allow whatever is occurring in the present moment to come and go."*

Step 3—Discuss
Say, *"Because we will be focusing on the present moment, let's talk a little about how long some of these things actually last: sounds, physical sensations, thoughts, etc."*

At this point, you can lead a whole-group discussion or have students talk in small groups and record their observations on the Open Awareness Activity Sheet. Students can do mini-experiments.

You might lead them through an example: Say, *"Notice a sound. Did you notice when the sound appeared and left? Was it near or far, loud or soft? Did it come and go one time, or over and over again? You can do the same with a thought, or physical sensation. What are the qualities of each aspect of your attention? Get curious about what is actually occurring in the present moment, rather than our thoughts about what is happening."*

The important concept for students to learn in this activity is that sounds, thoughts, feelings, and physical sensations do not last nearly as long as we might think they do. When we really attend to what is occurring we find that each of these aspects of awareness come and go, and what makes them seem to last longer is our thoughts about the experiences and sensations. This is the basis for the open awareness practice. Although it may be challenging at first for students to conceptualize the transitory nature of thoughts, feelings, physical sensations, sounds, etc., they will become more skillful as they practice.

Step 4—Practice
Say, *"Let's practice Strategy #5: Open Awareness Practice."*

Use the script verbatim, modify it to fit your own voice/word choice, or play the audio recording.

Step 5—Generalize
Say, *"This culminating open awareness practice incorporates aspects of the previous mindfulness practices we have learned. You can choose to focus on one aspect of the present moment, or open your awareness a bit wider to include many aspects of your direct experience. This formal practice can have positive effects on your daily life because if you learn how to attend to what is actually occurring right now, you might find that you are not spending as much time thinking or worrying about the past or future. This open awareness practice can also help you respond more skillfully to whatever is happening, rather than reacting mindlessly or carelessly."*

Remind them that the purpose of this particular practice is not to experience things in any certain way, but just as the sounds, sensations, thoughts, etc. occur in the present moment. Good or bad. You may ask students to practice this informally, maybe when they are riding the bus or in a car, or lying in bed. You can check back in with them later in the week to see what they observed.

Script for Open Awareness Practice

For this last strategy, you are going to practice bringing your awareness to whatever is occurring in the present moment (sounds, physical sensations, thoughts, feelings). Take a moment to get comfortable in an upright, seated posture, checking in with your body, relaxing if possible, and closing your eyes if that feels okay, or just lowering your gaze.

(Pause)

Begin by bringing awareness to your breath and the physical sensations in your body. Just noticing what your body feels like right now, not to change anything, just to know what is here. In this practice, we can explore different things occurring in the present moment. You can think about this practice as gradually widening the lens or focus of our attention. At its most focused point, we notice the sensations of breathing, but as we continue, we can attend to more aspects of our direct experience in the present moment. If at any time you become distracted or lost in thought, you can use that as an opportunity to begin again, by focusing just on the breath and the sensation of breathing in your body, or a wider, more open awareness of other aspects of the present moment.

(Pause)

You can choose to stay with your breath, or shift your awareness to the physical sensations in your body. Notice what is here. Is there pain or discomfort, openness and ease? What qualities do you notice? Temperature, texture, etc. You might be aware of when a physical sensation arises, stays for some time, and then gradually fades away. Just take a few moments to bring awareness to physical sensations in your body.

(Pause)

Next, if you choose, shift your awareness to sounds. You might hear sounds in the room, or outside of the room. Near or far, loud or soft. A sound may be constant for some time, and other sounds may come and go. In this practice, we are not trying to hear particular sounds, but rather letting our awareness be open to whatever sounds are here in the present moment.

(Pause)

Next, you can bring your attention to your thoughts and feelings. Just like with the sounds, we are not trying to think or feel any particular way, but just notice what occurs in our minds moment to moment. A thought may pop into your head, stay for a while, then leave. You may notice a pattern of thoughts or feelings. Simply allow the thoughts and feelings to arise and disappear as they naturally do. You may notice that you get stuck on a particular thought, or the same thought keeps occurring. This is okay. Just be aware what is happening here and now.

(Pause)

Finally, you may choose to open your awareness to include all of the aspects of your direct, present-moment experience. You can allow yourself to receive any sounds, physical sensations, thoughts, and/or feelings, occurring in the present moment. Again, you might think of your mind like a clear blue sky. Just like clouds come and go, so too do sounds, sensations in the body, thoughts, etc.

(Pause)

Gently bring your awareness back into this room. You may want to take a few deep breaths, inhaling and exhaling slowly and deeply. When you are ready, you can open your eyes. Practicing Open Awareness gives you a few moments of quiet time to focus on the present moment, and it can serve as a foundation for a skillful way to **respond** *to what is occurring actually in your life, rather than* **reacting** *to thoughts or feelings we may have about what is occurring.*

Enjoy the rest of your day.

OPEN AWARENESS
Sounds. Sensations. Thoughts. Feelings.

© 2019 Taylor & Francis

OPEN AWARENESS GROUP ACTIVITY

1. Notice **sounds** in the environment. What do you hear? Are they near or far? Loud or soft? Annoying or relaxing? Explore sounds you hear. Are they all the same? Do they stay forever or come and go?

2. Now notice **physical sensations** in your body. Maybe you have an itch, or notice your stomach growling.

3. Next, notice your **thoughts or feelings**. Where do they come from? Where do they go? How long do they stick around? Can you make them come and go, or do they come and go on their own?

4. Do you notice any patterns or surprises about the sounds, physical sensations or thoughts you have experienced during this activity?

© 2019 Taylor & Francis

 RESOURCES

 MYND TIME

This certificate is awarded to

in recognition of

PRACTICING OPEN AWARENESS

"Come from a space of peace and you will find that you can deal with anything."
- Michael Singer

_____
Signature

_____
Date

© 2019 Taylor & Francis

Epilogue

I have dedicated my life's work to helping educators realize their incredible potential, power, and purpose. It is my hope that after implementing *Mynd Time* in your classroom or another educational setting, you have found these foundational mindfulness practices to be both professionally and personally valuable. I encourage you to continue a personal daily practice, or if you have not established a daily practice, begin today. If you miss a few days, weeks or months, begin again. Be kind to yourself. We are all busy, doing the best we can. The practice of beginning again is a gentle way to bring awareness to the present moment. It does not matter how many times we forget or fall off track. Begin again.

You have taken multiple important steps toward fostering a positive, peaceful learning environment, where your students have increased their self-awareness and self-regulation. First, you explored how you might incorporate mindfulness in your personal and professional life. Second, you made the conscious decision to bring mindfulness into your classroom. Third, you prioritized your instructional time to include frequent practice opportunities for your students. These are no small feats. We do not always give ourselves credit for our positive actions yet what you have accomplished by implementing *Mynd Time* is praiseworthy. Take a few moments to acknowledge the incredible effort you have made to support your students' and your own well-being over the past few weeks and months.

The sources of stress within the school building are numerous. No mindfulness practice can make them disappear, but what you may find is that with a regular mindfulness practice, you do not feel as overwhelmed by the demands of public education (e.g., teacher evaluations, testing, changing standards, student issues, etc.). Mindfulness practices can do two things:

1) help you focus on the factors in your life that you have control over rather than spending a lot of time on things outside of your control, and 2) change your relationships with the stressors in your life (i.e. responding to people, situations, etc. rather than reacting mindlessly).

Almost every educator I have ever met has a heart-felt desire to help children reach their greatest potential. Education is a helping profession, much like counseling or nursing. In these helping careers, professionals often report feeling overwhelmed and emotionally and physically drained by the demands of the job, and feel as if they spend all of their time helping other people, with little to no energy left to tend to their own basic needs. One of the greatest gifts you can give your students is to prioritize your own self-care in the form of the mindfulness practices. When you take time to sit quietly and practice any of the mindfulness strategies, you become more skillful in self-awareness, self-regulation and in your ability to respond, rather than react to people and situations throughout the day. My hope is that you continue to dedicate time to helping your students increase their capacity to experience joy in the present moment, and that you also give yourself the same gift of time to enjoy all that this life has to offer.

References

American Federation of Teachers. (2017). *2017 Educator quality of work life survey.* Available from: www.aft.org/2017-educator-quality-life-survey (retrieved 7-18-18).

American Psychological Association. (2017). *Stress in America.* Available from: www.apa.org/news/press/releases/stress/ (retrieved 5-25-18).

Durlak, J., Weissberg, R., Dymnicki, A., Taylor, R., & Schellinger, K. (2011). The impact of enhancing students' social emotional learning: A meta-analysis of school-based universal interventions. *Child Development, 82*(1), 405–32.

Greenberg, M., Weissberg, R., et al. (2003). Enhancing school-based prevention and youth development through coordinated social, emotional, and academic learning. *American Psychologist, 58*(6–7), 466–74.

Hanson, R. (2009). *Buddha's brain.* Oakland, CA: New Harbinger.

Kabat-Zinn, J. (1994). *Wherever you go, there you are: Mindfulness meditation in everyday life.* New York: Hyperion.

Kang, Y., Gray, J. R., & Dovidio, J. F. (2014). The nondiscriminating heart: Loving-kindness meditation training decreases implicit intergroup bias. *Journal of Experimental Psychology, 143*(3), 1306–13.

Klimecki, O. M., Leiberg, S., Lamm, C., & Singer, T. (2013). Functional neural plasticity and associated changes in positive affect after compassion training. *Cerebral Cortex, 23*(7), 1552–61.

Kok, B. E., Coffey, K. A., Cohn, M. A., Catalino, L. I., Vacharkulksemsuk, T., Algoe, S. B., Brantley, M., & Fredrickson, B. L. (2013). How positive emotions build physical health: perceived positive social connections account for the upward spiral between positive emotions and vagal tone. *Psychological Science, 23*(7), 1123–32.

Shahar, B., Szsepsenwol, O., Zilcha-Mano, S., Haim, N., Zamir, O., Levi-Yeshuvi, S., & Levit-Binnun, N. (2015). A wait-list randomized controlled trial of loving-kindness meditation programme for self-criticism. *Clinical Psychology & Psychotherapy, 22*(4), 346–56.

Siegel, D., & Bryson, T. (2011). *The whole-brain child.* New York: Bantam Books.

Zins, J. E., Weissberg, R. P., Wang, M. C., & Walberg, H. J. (Eds.). (2004). *Building academic success through social and emotional learning: What does the research say?* New York: Teachers College Press.

For Product Safety Concerns and Information please contact our EU
representative GPSR@taylorandfrancis.com
Taylor & Francis Verlag GmbH, Kaufingerstraße 24, 80331 München, Germany

www.ingramcontent.com/pod-product-compliance
Lightning Source LLC
Chambersburg PA
CBHW081423230426
43668CB00016B/2329